Dear Parent:
Your child's love

Every child learns to read in a different way and at his or her own speed. Some go back and forth between reading levels and read favorite books again and again. Others read through each level in order. You can help your young reader improve and become more confident by encouraging his or her own interests and abilities. From books your child reads with you to the first books he or she reads alone, there are I Can Read Books for every stage of reading:

SHARED READING
Basic language, word repetition, and whimsical illustrations, ideal for sharing with your emergent reader

BEGINNING READING
Short sentences, familiar words, and simple concepts for children eager to read on their own

READING WITH HELP
Engaging stories, longer sentences, and language play for developing readers

READING ALONE
Complex plots, challenging vocabulary, and high-interest topics for the independent reader

ADVANCED READING
Short paragraphs, chapters, and exciting themes for the perfect bridge to chapter books

I Can Read Books have introduced children to the joy of reading since 1957. Featuring award-winning authors and illustrators and a fabulous cast of beloved characters, I Can Read Books set the standard for beginning readers.

A lifetime of discovery begins with the magical words **"I Can Read!"**

Visit www.icanread.com for information on enriching your child's reading experience.

For Debbie & Jesse, a couple of cake takers!
—H. P.

To Tanja for all her generosity of time, know-how, and spirit. Many thanks!
—L. A.

Gouache and black pencil were used to prepare the full-color art.

I Can Read Book® is a trademark of HarperCollins Publishers.

Amelia Bedelia is a registered trademark of Peppermint Partners, LLC.

 Printed in the U.S.A. For information address HarperCollins Children's Books, a division of HarperCollins Publishers, 195 Broadway, New York, NY 10007.
www.icanread.com

Library of Congress Cataloging-in-Publication Data is available.

ISBN 978-0-06-233431-2 (hardback)—ISBN 978-0-06-233430-5 (pbk)

16 17 18 19 20 LSCC 10 9 8 7 6 5 4 3 First Edition

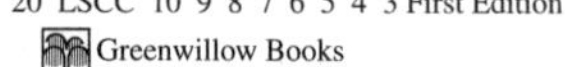

Amelia Bedelia

• Takes the Cake •

by Herman Parish ✿ pictures by Lynne Avril

Greenwillow Books, *An Imprint of* HarperCollins*Publishers*

SUPPORT OUR
ALL $'s for
Bake Sale
Bucks for Books

Amelia Bedelia and her classmates were having a bake sale.
The bake sale would raise money to help the library at their school buy new books.

“My mom helped me make an angel food cake,” said Angel.

Amelia Bedelia thought everything Angel ate was angel food.

"I made chocolate chip brownies," said Chip.

"Of course," said Amelia Bedelia. She was excited to share the super chewy brownies she had made.

Just then, Wade arrived with brownies.

So did Dawn and Holly and Heather.

Teddy and Clay brought brownies, too.

So did the rest of the class.

“Guys,” said Chip.

“This is a bake sale,

not a brownie festival.”

Miss Edwards, their teacher,
arrived with a big glass jar
to hold the money
from the sale.
"My goodness," she said.
"I've seen lots of mix-ups,
but this takes the cake."

“Please do not take our cake!”

said Amelia Bedelia.

“It’s the only one we’ve got.”

“Don’t worry. I’ll buy the cake,” said Miss Edwards. “I have plans for it!”

“Thank you,” said Angel. She put the money from Miss Edwards in the big glass jar.

"Go ahead and get set up,"

said Miss Edwards.

"I'll be back."

Amelia Bedelia and her classmates stared at stacks of brownies.

“Maybe we should put out a few at a time,” said Dawn.

Clay and Teddy gave her idea a try.

"That looks weird," said Wade.

"We did a lot of baking,

but I do not think we will sell a lot."

"I know," said Amelia Bedelia.

"Let's put them

all out at once!"

The brownies were all square.

They were all about the same size.

But the light, cakey ones were tall.

The dark, chewy ones were short.

Some had flaky tops.

Others were smooth and flat.

Teddy had put icing on his batch.

Holly had dusted her batch with powdered sugar.

The bakers stood back
to admire their work.
"That looks amazing," said Penny.
"I've never seen so much chocolate."

"It's cool," said Skip.
"They are the same
but also not the same."

Cliff squinted his eyes.

"Too bad we can't make one big brownie!" he said.

"We could set a world record for biggest brownie."

Amelia Bedelia squinted her eyes.

She could see what Cliff saw.

She also saw something else.

She began moving brownies

here and there

and everywhere.

Amelia Bedelia stood back
to admire her work.
"Now that is one big brown 'E'!"
she said.

Everyone laughed and cheered.

"That is amazing," said Angel.

"We need new signs," said Clay.

Everyone got to work.

Homemade GOODIES!
SCHOOL BU
BROWN "E" Books = YUM!
Biggest BROWN "E" in town!! Spell with chocolate!

Soon, kids from other classes came to the bake sale.

Parents and babysitters stopped by.

So did teachers and bus drivers.

The principal and the school nurse visited, too.

Everyone wanted a taste of the biggest brown "E" in town.

"Wow!" said Miss Edwards.
"I've been to many bake sales,
but this really does take the cake!"

“No, you bought the cake!”
said Amelia Bedelia.
“I did,” said Miss Edwards.
“I thought the best bakers in town
might like a snack
when their work was done.”

"Thanks, Miss Edwards," said Angel.
She was trying to smile.
"I do like angel food cakes,
but I really wanted to try a brownie.
We sold out before I got a taste."
"Well, you can't have your cake
and eat it, too," said Miss Edwards.

"What good is having a cake
if you can't eat it?"
said Amelia Bedelia.

"Good point," said Miss Edwards.
She cut the cake into even slices.

Everyone enjoyed the treat.
This time, they could
have their cake
and eat it, too!

Dear Parent:
Your child's love of reading starts here!

Every child learns to read in a different way and at his or her own speed. Some go back and forth between reading levels and read favorite books again and again. Others read through each level in order. You can help your young reader improve and become more confident by encouraging his or her own interests and abilities. From books your child reads with you to the first books he or she reads alone, there are I Can Read Books for every stage of reading:

SHARED READING
Basic language, word repetition, and whimsical illustrations, ideal for sharing with your emergent reader

BEGINNING READING
Short sentences, familiar words, and simple concepts for children eager to read on their own

READING WITH HELP
Engaging stories, longer sentences, and language play for developing readers

READING ALONE
Complex plots, challenging vocabulary, and high-interest topics for the independent reader

ADVANCED READING
Short paragraphs, chapters, and exciting themes for the perfect bridge to chapter books

I Can Read Books have introduced children to the joy of reading since 1957. Featuring award-winning authors and illustrators and a fabulous cast of beloved characters, I Can Read Books set the standard for beginning readers.

A lifetime of discovery begins with the magical words **"I Can Read!"**

Visit www.icanread.com for information on enriching your child's reading experience.

Sumaya and Roger chalk up another one!
—H. P.

For Skip and Debbie, with love
—L. A.

Gouache and black pencil were used to prepare the full-color art.

Library of Congress Cataloging-in-Publication Data

Parish, Herman.
Amelia Bedelia chalks one up / Herman Parish ; pictures by Lynne Avril.
pages cm—(I can read. Level 1)
"Greenwillow Books."
Summary: Amelia Bedelia wants her mother to stop feeling blue. She suggests Mom go on a playdate while Amelia Bedelia is doing the same, and then enlists her friends to help make chalk drawings on the house, sidewalk, and more to brighten Mom's day with her favorite things.
ISBN 978-0-06-233422-0 (hardback)—ISBN 978-0-06-233421-3 (pbk.) [1. Mood (Psychology)—Fiction.
2. Drawing—Fiction. 3. Mothers and daughters—Fiction. 4. Humorous stories.] I. Avril, Lynne, (date) illustrator. II. Title.
PZ7.P2185Aob 2014 [E]—dc23 2014010789

16 17 18 19 20 LSCC 10 9 8 First Edition

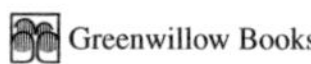 Greenwillow Books

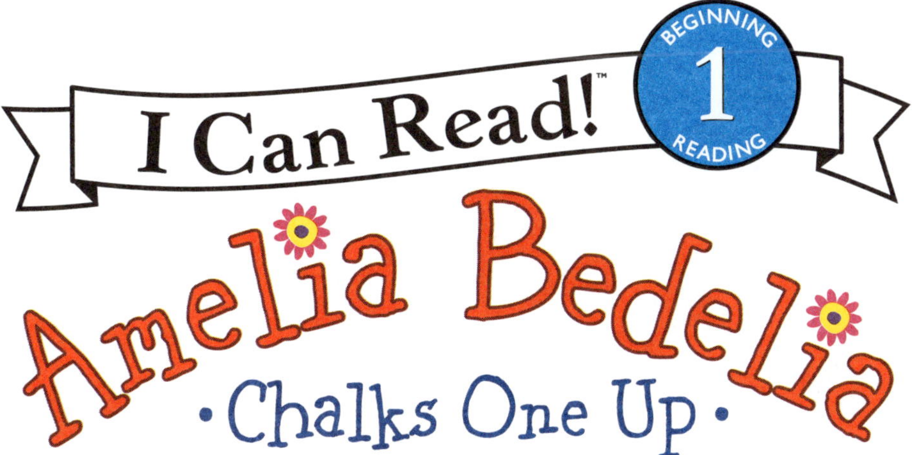

by Herman Parish pictures by Lynne Avril

Greenwillow Books, *An Imprint of* HarperCollins*Publishers*

Amelia Bedelia's mother
was as glum as the weather.
"Where is the sun?" she asked.
"I am really blue."

Amelia Bedelia looked at her mother.

She was not blue.

She was not even wearing anything blue.

She was not wearing a smile, either.

“I am having a playdate,”

said Amelia Bedelia.

“Maybe you should have one, too.”

"Great idea, sweetie!"
said Amelia Bedelia's mom.
She made two short phone calls.

Then she said,

"I am going to town.

After I go shopping,

I will meet Dad for coffee.

Mrs. Adams will watch you and Rose."

"Have fun," said Mrs. Adams,

who was their next-door neighbor.

"Don't worry about us girls.

We will have a ball."

Amelia Bedelia's mother
waved good-bye.
"Well, chalk up another gray day!"
she said.
As Amelia Bedelia waved back,
she got an even better idea.

Amelia Bedelia found her big bucket of chalk in the garage.

When Rose's father dropped Rose off, Amelia Bedelia was already hard at work.

"Wow!" said Rose. "You have every color in the rainbow!"

“I need them,” said Amelia Bedelia.

“I’m chalking up a gray day

to make my mom happy.

Want to help?”

“Sure!” said Rose.

To warm up their drawing arms,
Amelia Bedelia and Rose drew
squares for hopscotch
on the sidewalk.
When they played a game,
Mrs. Adams was amazing!

Chip walked by with his big brother and their puppy, Scout.

"What is going on?" yelled Chip.

"We're chalking up a gray day," said Amelia Bedelia.

"Want to help?"

"Cool!" said Chip.

"What makes your mom happy?"
asked Rose.
"She likes flowers and green things,"
said Amelia Bedelia,
pointing to where plants grew last year.

Rose got green, red, and pink chalk.
She began drawing roses
on Amelia Bedelia's house.

“Hey, Amelia Bedelia!”

Daisy was walking by

with her babysitter

and her baby sister.

“What are you doing?” she asked.

“Chalking up a gray day,”

said Amelia Bedelia.

“Want to help?”

“Yes!” said Daisy.

Daisy began drawing daisies.

"That's my mom's favorite flower,"

said Amelia Bedelia.

"She will love those.

Thanks!"

Amelia Bedelia told her friends
about her mom's favorite spots.
Chip drew a map.
Amelia Bedelia, Rose, and Daisy
added shops and places to eat.

YOGA STUDIO
SHOES GALORE
Blooms
omplete
offee shop
Barb's
Bakery
Mrs. B's Books
enny
allery
Statement
HAIR AFFAIR

Mrs. Adams made tasty treats
for everyone.
"What great drawings," she said.
"Roll out the red carpet for your mom!"

Amelia Bedelia didn’t have one.

So they drew her mom a carpet

leading to the best surprise of all.

Then Amelia Bedelia saw their car pulling into the driveway.

Her parents had come home together.

"Hi, Mom!" said Amelia Bedelia. "Welcome back!"

“You guys really went to town,”

said Amelia Bedelia’s father.

“Not us,” said Amelia Bedelia.

“Mom went to town.

We stayed home and drew!”

Amelia Bedelia's parents
followed the red carpet.
Everyone else followed them.
"A yellow sun plus a blue mom
makes green," said Amelia Bedelia.
"And green makes you happy."

Amelia Bedelia's mother
was speechless.
She hugged each of them.
She hugged Amelia Bedelia
the longest of all.
Amelia Bedelia's dad
took more photographs.
It was a good thing he did.

It rained all night long.
The chalk washed away,
and the pictures melted.
All the colors of the rainbow
soaked into the earth.

The next day was bright and sunny.
Amelia Bedelia and her mom
stood at the window
feeling yellow and pink and green
and every other color . . . except blue.

Dear Parent:
Your child's love of reading starts here!

Every child learns to read in a different way and at his or her own speed. Some go back and forth between reading levels and read favorite books again and again. Others read through each level in order. You can help your young reader improve and become more confident by encouraging his or her own interests and abilities. From books your child reads with you to the first books he or she reads alone, there are I Can Read Books for every stage of reading:

SHARED READING
Basic language, word repetition, and whimsical illustrations, ideal for sharing with your emergent reader

BEGINNING READING
Short sentences, familiar words, and simple concepts for children eager to read on their own

READING WITH HELP
Engaging stories, longer sentences, and language play for developing readers

READING ALONE
Complex plots, challenging vocabulary, and high-interest topics for the independent reader

ADVANCED READING
Short paragraphs, chapters, and exciting themes for the perfect bridge to chapter books

I Can Read Books have introduced children to the joy of reading since 1957. Featuring award-winning authors and illustrators and a fabulous cast of beloved characters, I Can Read Books set the standard for beginning readers.

A lifetime of discovery begins with the magical words **"I Can Read!"**

Visit www.icanread.com for information on enriching your child's reading experience.

For Angelina—"Just my lucky!"
—H. P.

To Cortney, Tyson, Mayson, and Jonah,
I'm lucky to have you for neighbors!
—L. A.

Gouache and black pencil were used to prepare the full-color art.

I Can Read Book® is a trademark of HarperCollins Publishers.
Amelia Bedelia is a registered trademark of Peppermint Partners, LLC.

 Printed in the U.S.A. For information address HarperCollins Children's Books, a division of HarperCollins Publishers, 195 Broadway, New York, NY 10007.
www.icanread.com

Library of Congress Cataloging-in-Publication Data

Parish, Herman.
Amelia Bedelia tries her luck / by Herman Parish ; pictures by Lynne Avril.
pages cm.—(I can read! 1, Beginning reading)
Summary: "Amelia Bedelia turns bad luck into good luck"—Provided by publisher.
ISBN 978-0-06-222128-5 (trade ed. : alk. paper)—ISBN 978-0-06-222127-8 (pbk. : alk. paper) [1. Luck—Fiction. 2. Humorous stories.] I. Avril, Lynne, (date), illustrator. II. Title.
PZ7.P2185Ard 2013 [E]—dc23 2013033228

16 17 18 19 20 LSCC 10 9 8 First Edition

Greenwillow Books

by Herman Parish pictures by Lynne Avril

Greenwillow Books, *An Imprint of* HarperCollins*Publishers*

SCHOOL BUS

Amelia Bedelia was getting ready to go to school when . . .

CRASH!

"I'm sorry!" said Amelia Bedelia.

"Accidents happen, sweetie,"

said her mother.

"The important thing

is that you are not hurt."

At school, Amelia Bedelia told her friends about the accident.

“You’re in trouble,” said Clay.

“Breaking a mirror means

seven years of bad luck.”

“Seven years!”

said Amelia Bedelia.

“That’s almost my whole life!”

"Even worse," said Rose.

"Today is Friday the thirteenth.

Bad luck gets doubled today."

"That's fourteen years!"

said Amelia Bedelia.

"I'll have bad luck forever!"

“Amelia Bedelia,” said Joy, “you can change your luck.”

“That’s right,” said Heather. “My dad always says,

See a penny, pick it up,

all the day you’ll have good luck.”

Amelia Bedelia picked up Penny.

"Put me down!" said Penny.

"Heather means a penny coin,

not a Penny person."

At recess, the whole class tried to help Amelia Bedelia change her luck.

They searched for a four-leaf clover.

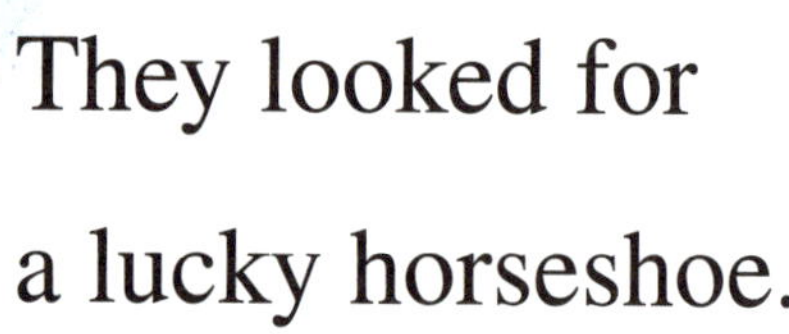

They looked for a lucky horseshoe.

They tried to find a rabbit's foot.

The playground didn't have any of those things.

"I'm sorry, Amelia Bedelia," said Clay. "We struck out. You are out of luck."

Amelia Bedelia made a plan.
If she could not find luck,
she would make her own luck.

Two Rabbit's Feet =
Double Luck

12 Leaf Clover =
3 x
Luck

ur Horseshoes =
4 x Luck

Amelia Bedelia's teacher, Miss Edwards, saw her drawings.

She also saw that Amelia Bedelia was upset.

"Are you all right?" asked Miss Edwards.

"No, I am all wrong,"
said Amelia Bedelia.
She told Miss Edwards
about breaking the mirror
and her double bad luck.

“Amelia Bedelia,” said Miss Edwards,
“today is my lucky day.
Friday the thirteenth
is the perfect day
to talk about luck.”

The class listed lucky and unlucky things.

They talked about bad luck and good luck.

There were all kinds of questions.

Supers
Bad Luck
Breaking a mirror
Black cat crosses your path
Walking under a ladder
(not unlucky, just dangerous)

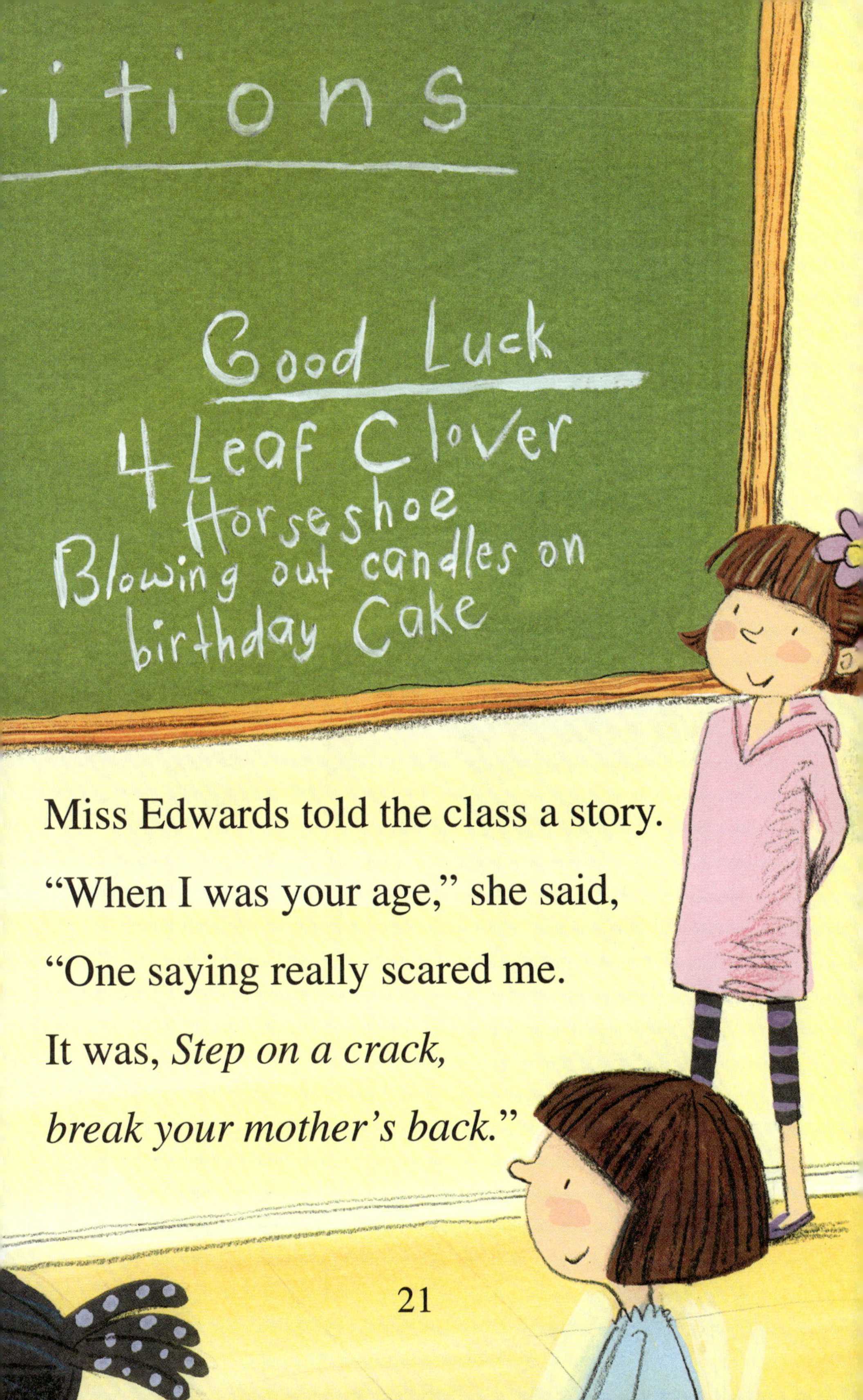

Miss Edwards told the class a story.

"When I was your age," she said,

"One saying really scared me.

It was, *Step on a crack,*

break your mother's back."

"That's terrible," said Amelia Bedelia.

"But it isn't true," said Miss Edwards.

"Just like breaking a mirror isn't bad luck."

“Breaking a mirror is bad luck,” said Clay.

“It’s bad luck for the mirror!”

Everyone laughed.

Amelia Bedelia laughed hardest of all.

She felt a lot better.

As Amelia Bedelia was walking home, she saw a crack in the sidewalk. "Bad luck? Ha!" she said.

She stepped on the crack. She stepped on every crack she saw. When she spied the biggest one of all, Amelia Bedelia stomped on it.

Then Amelia Bedelia turned onto her street, and she stopped in her tracks.

There was an ambulance
in front of her house.
Amelia Bedelia raced home.
Breaking the mirror was an accident,
but she had stepped on those cracks
on purpose.

“Mom!” yelled Amelia Bedelia.
“I didn’t mean to break your back!”

The ambulance was pulling away.

“Mom!” cried Amelia Bedelia. “Mom!”

"Amelia Bedelia!" said her mother.

"I'm with Mrs. Adams, sweetie."

Amelia Bedelia whirled around.

Her mom was with their neighbor.

Her back was fine!

Amelia Bedelia ran to her mom.

She gave her the biggest,

longest, strongest hug ever.

"Ouch, honey!"

said Amelia Bedelia's mother.

"Do you want to break my back?"

"No, never!" said Amelia Bedelia.

"You just missed the excitement," said Mrs. Adams. "I got a ride home in an ambulance after my checkup."

"Are you okay?" asked Amelia Bedelia. "I am fine," said Mrs. Adams. "Knock on wood."

Then Mrs. Adams knocked three times on her porch railing.

Tomorrow, Amelia Bedelia would add "knock on wood" to the list her class had made.

Today, worrying about luck had worn her out.

Amelia Bedelia thought about her family and her great friends. She thought that the mirror Mrs. Adams gave her was cool.

Amelia Bedelia felt like she was the luckiest person in the world.

Dear Parent:
Your child's love of reading starts here!

Every child learns to read in a different way and at his or her own speed. Some go back and forth between reading levels and read favorite books again and again. Others read through each level in order. You can help your young reader improve and become more confident by encouraging his or her own interests and abilities. From books your child reads with you to the first books he or she reads alone, there are I Can Read Books for every stage of reading:

SHARED READING
Basic language, word repetition, and whimsical illustrations, ideal for sharing with your emergent reader

BEGINNING READING
Short sentences, familiar words, and simple concepts for children eager to read on their own

READING WITH HELP
Engaging stories, longer sentences, and language play for developing readers

READING ALONE
Complex plots, challenging vocabulary, and high-interest topics for the independent reader

ADVANCED READING
Short paragraphs, chapters, and exciting themes for the perfect bridge to chapter books

I Can Read Books have introduced children to the joy of reading since 1957. Featuring award-winning authors and illustrators and a fabulous cast of beloved characters, I Can Read Books set the standard for beginning readers.

A lifetime of discovery begins with the magical words **"I Can Read!"**

Visit www.icanread.com for information on enriching your child's reading experience.

Leaf it to Fiona!
—H. P.

For Bunny and Paris
—L. A.

Gouache and black pencil were used to prepare the full-color art.

 Printed in the U.S.A. For information address HarperCollins Children's Books, a division of HarperCollins Publishers, 10 East 53rd Street, New York, NY 10022.
www.icanread.com

Library of Congress Cataloging-in-Publication Data

Parish, Herman.
Amelia Bedelia hits the trail / by Herman Parish ; illustrated by Lynne Avril.
p. cm.—(I can read! 1-beginning reading)
"Greenwillow Books."
Summary: On a nature hike with her class, young Amelia Bedelia's literal-mindedness causes confusion along with some laughs.
ISBN 978-0-06-209527-5 (hardback)—ISBN 978-0-06-209526-8 (pbk.) [1. Hiking—Fiction. 2. Nature study—Fiction. 3. School field trips—Fiction. 4. Humorous stories.] I. Avril, Lynne, (date) illustrator. II. Title. PZ7.P2185Aon 2013 [E]—dc23 2012036841

16 17 18 19 20 LSCC 10 First Edition

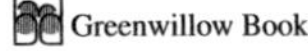
Greenwillow Books

by Herman Parish ✿ pictures by Lynne Avril

Greenwillow Books, *An Imprint of* HarperCollins*Publishers*

Amelia Bedelia was going hiking.
Her entire class was going, too.
"Let's hit the trail," said Miss Edwards,
Amelia Bedelia's teacher.

The trail was steep.

Everyone stepped over a big tree root.

Amelia Bedelia was chatting

and looking up at the birds and . . .

Amelia Bedelia fell flat on her face.

"Are you okay?" asked Miss Edwards.

"I'm okay," said Amelia Bedelia.

"But the next time I hit the trail,

I'll use this stick instead of my face!"

Amelia Bedelia and her friends spotted lots of living things along the trail.

They saw a deer
and a rabbit.

They saw squirrels
and chipmunks.

They saw insects
crawling along the ground

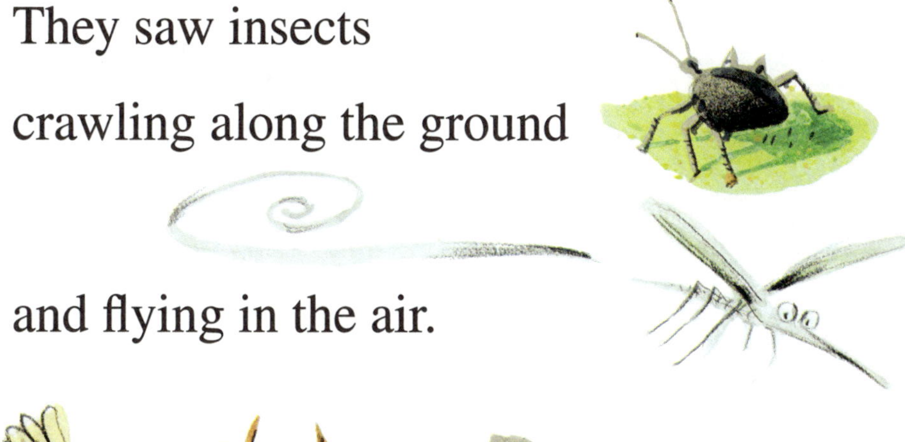

and flying in the air.

Birds chirped
in the trees.

When a snake crossed the trail,

Chip let out a yell.

"Relax," said Penny.

"It is more scared of you

than you are of it."

The class walked slowly.

“Let’s move a little faster,”

said Miss Edwards.

“Pick up your snail’s pace.”

Amelia Bedelia looked for a snail

with a pace to pick up.

Maybe she could find one

for the classroom nature table.

“I’m hungry,” said Clay.

“Can we eat lunch?”

Miss Edwards read her map.

“There is a stream ahead,” she said.

“We can stop there for a bite.”

“I have lots of bites,” said Amelia Bedelia.

"I can see water!" said Penny.

The class raced to the stream.

"We'll eat lunch on the bank.

Dig in!" said Miss Edwards.

Amelia Bedelia didn't see a bank,

or even a cash machine.

Was there treasure buried here?

Why else would Miss Edwards tell them to dig in?

It was time to go back to school.

Wade was the last to finish his lunch.

“Let’s go, Wade,” said Miss Edwards.

“Yay!” said Amelia Bedelia.

Amelia Bedelia took off
her shoes and socks
and waded right into the stream.

Soon everyone was splashing
with Amelia Bedelia.
Even Miss Edwards joined the fun.

As they walked back,
everyone found things
for the nature table.

Daisy picked a daisy.

Holly plucked
a sprig of holly.

Rose found
a wild rose.

Amelia Bedelia
picked up fallen leaves.

“What did you find, Amelia Bedelia?” asked Miss Edwards.

"These are my leafs," said Amelia Bedelia.

Miss Edwards smiled.

"When you have more than one leaf, you say *leaves*," she said.

That made sense to Amelia Bedelia.

In the fall, every leaf had to leave its tree.

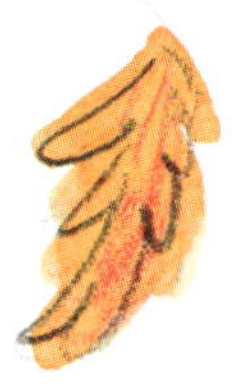

Amelia Bedelia knew
she would not think anymore
of a leaf falling off a tree.
She would think
it was leaving
its tree.

"Nice leaves," said Skip.

"You have maple,

oak,

and chestnut," he said.

Skip knew a lot about trees.

"What is this red one?"

asked Amelia Bedelia.

“Uh-oh,” said Skip. “That is poison ivy!”

YEE-AHHHH!!

Amelia Bedelia threw the leaves

up in the air.

Her leaves were leaving again!

Skip laughed so hard
he fell on the ground.
"I was joking!" he said.
Amelia Bedelia was not laughing.
"That was a mean trick," she said.

"Maybe you should take a hike," said Skip.

"I am," said Amelia Bedelia. "And now I don't have anything for the nature table."

Amelia Bedelia's lip trembled.

"I'm sorry, Amelia Bedelia," said Skip.

He helped Amelia Bedelia

pick up her leaves.

"Hold still!" Skip said.

"Are you teasing again?"

asked Amelia Bedelia.

“No. You have a hitchhiker,” said Skip.

He pointed at a caterpillar.

The caterpillar was crawling

on Amelia Bedelia’s backpack.

“Wow!” said Amelia Bedelia.

Amelia Bedelia's caterpillar

was the star of the nature table.

Then it was the star

of Amelia Bedelia's classroom . . .

1.
2.
3.

until it hit the trail.

Dear Parent:
Your child's love of reading starts here!

Every child learns to read in a different way and at his or her own speed. Some go back and forth between reading levels and read favorite books again and again. Others read through each level in order. You can help your young reader improve and become more confident by encouraging his or her own interests and abilities. From books your child reads with you to the first books he or she reads alone, there are I Can Read Books for every stage of reading:

SHARED READING
Basic language, word repetition, and whimsical illustrations, ideal for sharing with your emergent reader

BEGINNING READING
Short sentences, familiar words, and simple concepts for children eager to read on their own

READING WITH HELP
Engaging stories, longer sentences, and language play for developing readers

READING ALONE
Complex plots, challenging vocabulary, and high-interest topics for the independent reader

ADVANCED READING
Short paragraphs, chapters, and exciting themes for the perfect bridge to chapter books

I Can Read Books have introduced children to the joy of reading since 1957. Featuring award-winning authors and illustrators and a fabulous cast of beloved characters, I Can Read Books set the standard for beginning readers.

A lifetime of discovery begins with the magical words **"I Can Read!"**

Visit www.icanread.com for information on enriching your child's reading experience.

For Chris and Mara, who never *sleep*
—H. P.

For Rose–thanks for having it at your house!
—L. A.

Gouache and black pencil were used to prepare the full-color art.

I Can Read Book® is a trademark of HarperCollins Publishers.
Amelia Bedelia is a registered trademark of Peppermint Partners, LLC.

www.icanread.com

Library of Congress Cataloging-in-Publication Data

Parish, Herman.
Amelia Bedelia sleeps over / by Herman Parish ; pictures by Lynne Avril.
p. cm.—(I can read! 1-beginning reading)
"Greenwillow Books."
Summary: Amelia Bedelia has a wonderful time at her first slumber party.
ISBN 978-0-06-209524-4 (trade ed.)—ISBN 978-0-06-209523-7 (pbk.) [1. Sleepovers—Fiction. 2. Humorous stories.]
I. Avril, Lynne,(date) ill. II. Title. PZ7.P2185Aps 2012 [Fic]—dc23 2012006186

16 17 18 19 20 LSCC 20 19 18 17 16 First Edition

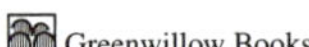

Greenwillow Books

Amelia Bedelia Sleeps Over

by Herman Parish ✿ pictures by Lynne Avril

Greenwillow Books, *An Imprint of* HarperCollins*Publishers*

Love

Amelia Bedelia was excited.
Tonight was her very first sleepover.
All the girls in her class
were going to Rose's house
for a slumber party.

Amelia Bedelia and her mother
drove to Rose's house.
"Is a slumber party fun?"
asked Amelia Bedelia.
"Because sleeping is boring."

"You might not sleep much,"
said her mother.
"You will play, eat pizza, paint nails . . ."

"Do we paint the nails
and then hammer them?"
asked Amelia Bedelia.

"Or do we hammer them first?"

Amelia Bedelia's mother laughed.
"You'll have fun, sweetie," she said.
"I promise."

When Amelia Bedelia arrived,
the front door swung open.
Her friends ran out to greet her.
Rose's mother came outside, too.

“Good luck,” said Amelia Bedelia’s mom.

“I think I’ll need it!” said Rose’s mother.

“I am a light sleeper.”

“Me too,” said Amelia Bedelia.
She reached into her backpack
and pulled out her flashlight.
“I sleep with this light every night.”

The girls played board games.
Amelia Bedelia had worried
that she would be bored,
but she was not.

Next, everyone went outside
and played tag
until the sun began to set.

“The pizza is here!” called Rose’s father. “Come and get it!”

“And for dessert,” said Rose’s mother, “we will toast marshmallows and make s’mores.”

“Won’t that wreck your toaster?”
asked Amelia Bedelia.
“Marshmallows melt into gooey, blobby . . .”

Rose’s father laughed.
“We’ll toast them on the grill,” he said.

After the pizza was gone,

Dawn speared a marshmallow

on Amelia Bedelia's stick.

Holly showed her how to turn it

carefully and slowly

to get a crunchy brown skin.

Amelia Bedelia put her marshmallow on top of a chocolate bar between two graham crackers.

"Yum!" said Amelia Bedelia. "I'd like some more, please!"

"Now you know why they're called s'mores!" said Rose.

After many more s'mores,
the girls went inside the house.
They put on their pajamas,
but it was not time to slumber yet.

Rose brought out bottles

of glittery nail polish

in more colors than the rainbow.

Every color had the perfect name.

Heather painted
Amelia Bedelia's nails

with
"Shamrock Green"
on her left hand,

"Blue Iceberg"
on her right hand,

and
"Banana Sunrise"
on her right foot.

She saved her left foot for
“Cotton Candy Cupcake.”

Amelia Bedelia sighed and said,
“I’m so happy
we don’t have to hammer them!”

Too soon, the clock struck ten.

"Bedtime, girls!" said Rose's mother.

"Lights out, and no giggling allowed!"

Oh well, thought Amelia Bedelia.

Here comes the slumber part

of this slumber party.

Off went the lights and lamps.

On went Amelia Bedelia's flashlight.

She showed her friends how to make

shadow puppets on the wall.

One by one,
the girls fell asleep.
All except Amelia Bedelia.

She was not one bit sleepy.
She made a rabbit.

Then a barking dog.

Then an elephant
with a trunk to grab . . .
Oops!
Her flashlight went out.
"Oh, no," said Amelia Bedelia.
What light would keep her company now?

Then Amelia Bedelia noticed
a very bright light
peeking into the family room.

She pulled back the curtains.
A full moon shone down on her.
Now there was too much light!

Amelia Bedelia dragged her sleeping bag under Rose's Ping-Pong table.

Perfect, thought Amelia Bedelia. Now I am having a sleepover and a sleep under.

Amelia Bedelia snuggled down into her cozy sleeping bag. She gazed up at the moon. She had heard people say that there was a man in the moon. She'd never seen him, until tonight.

He looked just like her dad.

Amelia Bedelia closed her eyes.

A second later, she was sound asleep.

The next morning,
the girls had a pillow fight.

Then they made chocolate chip pancakes

and helped to clean up the mess.

Amelia Bedelia's dad picked her up.

"Nice nails," said her father.

"Thanks, moon man," said Amelia Bedelia.

"Huh?" said her father.

"You sound like you need to take a nap."

And so Amelia Bedelia did,

all the way home.

Dear Parent: Your child's love of reading starts here!

Every child learns to read in a different way and at his or her own speed. Some go back and forth between reading levels and read favorite books again and again. Others read through each level in order. You can help your young reader improve and become more confident by encouraging his or her own interests and abilities. From books your child reads with you to the first books he or she reads alone, there are I Can Read Books for every stage of reading:

SHARED READING
Basic language, word repetition, and whimsical illustrations, ideal for sharing with your emergent reader

BEGINNING READING
Short sentences, familiar words, and simple concepts for children eager to read on their own

READING WITH HELP
Engaging stories, longer sentences, and language play for developing readers

READING ALONE
Complex plots, challenging vocabulary, and high-interest topics for the independent reader

ADVANCED READING
Short paragraphs, chapters, and exciting themes for the perfect bridge to chapter books

I Can Read Books have introduced children to the joy of reading since 1957. Featuring award-winning authors and illustrators and a fabulous cast of beloved characters, I Can Read Books set the standard for beginning readers.

A lifetime of discovery begins with the magical words **"I Can Read!"**

Visit www.icanread.com for information on enriching your child's reading experience.

For Roger & Sumaya—best buds
—H. P.

To all my old and new best friends
—L. A.

 Printed in the United States of America. Gouache and black pencil were used to prepare the full-color art. For information address HarperCollins Children's Books, a division of HarperCollins Publishers, 195 Broadway, New York, NY 10007.

www.icanread.com

Library of Congress Cataloging-in-Publication Data

Parish, Herman.

Amelia Bedelia makes a friend / by Herman Parish ; pictures by Lynne Avril.

p. cm. — (I can read! 1 beginning reading)

Summary: When her best friend moves out of the house next door, Amelia Bedelia wonders who the new neighbors will be.

ISBN 978-0-06-207516-1 (trade ed.) — ISBN 978-0-06-207515-4 (pbk. ed.) [1. Best friends—Fiction. 2. Friendship—Fiction. 3. Neighbors—Fiction.] I. Avril, Lynne, ill. II. Title. PZ7.P2185Ap 2012 [E]—dc23 2011018415

16 17 18 19 20 LSCC 20 19 18 17 16 First Edition

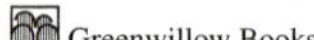 Greenwillow Books

Amelia Bedelia

·Makes a Friend·

by Herman Parish ✿ pictures by Lynne Avril

Greenwillow Books, *An Imprint of* HarperCollins*Publishers*

Amelia Bedelia was lucky.

Her best friend lived next door.

“Hello, Jen!” said Amelia Bedelia.

“Hi, Amelia Bedelia!” said Jen.

Amelia Bedelia and Jen

had been friends

since they were babies.

They baked together.

They dressed up together.

They played music together.

Amelia Bedelia even showed Jen how to bowl.

“They play so well together,”
said Amelia Bedelia’s mother.
“They sure do,” said Jen’s mother.
“Even though they are
as different as night and day.”

Then one day,
Jen and her parents
moved away.
Amelia Bedelia and her parents
were very sad.

Amelia Bedelia missed Jen.

She missed Jen every day.

She wished Jen would come back.

One morning, a moving van pulled up.

"Did Jen come back?"

asked Amelia Bedelia.

"I don't think so,"

said Amelia Bedelia's mother.

"We must have new neighbors."

Amelia Bedelia's mother watched the movers. "Oh, look," she said. "I see a fancy footstool."

Amelia Bedelia did not look. She wanted Jen back.

“Look!” said Amelia Bedelia’s mother.

“I see a coffee table.”

Amelia Bedelia still did not look.

She just kept drawing.

Amelia Bedelia's mother said, "I see some big armchairs."

"I see a loveseat."

"I see a twin bed."

Finally, Amelia Bedelia looked at Jen's old house. Then she looked at her drawings. "Our new neighbors sound strange," she said.

That night, Amelia Bedelia
told her dad
about the new neighbors.

He loved her pictures.

“Amazing!” her dad said.

“I hope they have a pool table.”

The next morning,
Amelia Bedelia and her mother
baked blueberry muffins.

They took the muffins
next door.

A lady opened the door.

"Hello there," she said.

"My name is Mrs. Adams.

You must be my new neighbors."

"No," said Amelia Bedelia.
"We already live here.
You are my new neighbor."

"You know," said Mrs. Adams,

"I think both of us are right.

Do come in."

"Mmmm," Mrs. Adams said.

"What smells so good?"

"My mom does," said Amelia Bedelia.

"I don't wear perfume yet."

Jen's house looked different.
Every room was full of boxes.
"Welcome to my mess,"
said Mrs. Adams.
"I will live out of boxes for a while."
That sounded fun to Amelia Bedelia.

"Are the twins in their bed?"

asked Amelia Bedelia.

"My goodness," said Mrs. Adams.

"You have sharp eyes."

Amelia Bedelia hoped that was good.

“My twin grandchildren
will visit today,” said Mrs. Adams.
“Their names are Mary and Marty.”

The twins visited that afternoon.

"Our grandma is a lot of fun,"

they told Amelia Bedelia.

They were right!

It was great to have a friend

right next door again.

Amelia Bedelia and Mrs. Adams baked together.

They dressed up together.

They played music together.

"They have so much fun together,"
said Amelia Bedelia's father.
"They sure do,"
said Amelia Bedelia's mother.
"Even though they are
as different as night and day."

One day Jen came back to visit.
Mrs. Adams took both girls
to a real bowling alley.

"This is the best day ever,"

said Amelia Bedelia.

"I have a best old friend

and a best new friend.

We are three best friends together!"